CHOOSE WISELY

RAISING UP WISE WOMEN OF GOD

NEHA EVANS FRANCIS

ISBN 979-8-88555-108-3

This book is dedicated with love to my husband, Evans, who has consistently given me more than I ever prayed for. You and I both know prayer works.

Contents

Introduction

If you want to stay happy, you must make the right choices about God, friends, education, and your life partner. Sure enough, if you make the wrong choices in these areas, you will live in misery. You will waste your energy hating your job, and that will do no good for your career or life. You will be stuck in the wrong place doing something boring. In the end, it will affect not only your professional life but also your personal life. So, you must be smart when making important life decisions. How can you do this? By listening to the Holy Spirit.

Are you surrounded by the clamour of conversation and dialogue? How can you discern the Holy Spirit's guidance through all the noise you experience in life?

In this book, I will share how you can make wise choices in different aspects of your life and decide whether they will be suitable for you in the long run or not.

Yes, planning is a time-consuming affair but to enjoy a successful and happy life, you must tread that path circumspectly. It is definitely worth the time and effort because choosing wisely will pay dividends in your life.

In Christ,

Neha Evans Francis

Foreword

It is a pleasure for me to write this foreword for my wife's wonderful book *Choose Wisely*. It has been seven years since I have known her personally, and during this time, I saw her making many decisions, some casually and others wisely. One of the most important decisions she made was to marry me. It was not an easy decision, but she was obedient to God, took that plunge, and today, she is glad she did it.

I could see a burden on her, unlike some young girls who destroy their lives by making foolish decisions. This book is the outcome of that burden, which God gave her.

Being in full-time ministry for over eleven years, I can say I have received more calls from young women than young men concerning choices. Most of them messed up their lives because of poor decision-making. They chose the wrong God, wrong friend, or a wrong life partner.

I believe this book will enlighten any young girl to make sound decisions in the most important areas of her life. It is not just easy to read and follow, but it has also been carefully curated with the best advice I know from someone who has become wise by learning from the wrong turns she made.

I am so glad to have Neha in my life. I cannot imagine what it would be like without a praying wife. It gives me comfort and security and also fulfils the mission the Lord has for us to pray for each other and bear one another's burdens. I can think of no better way to truly love your husband than by lifting him up in prayer on a consistent basis. It is a priceless gift that helps us experience God's blessings and grace. Neha, I love you.

Your covered-in-prayer husband,
Evans Francis

Connect with Evans Francis

WhatsApp: https://wa.me/919960877313

YouTube: www.youtube.com/evansfrancis

Facebook: https://www.facebook.com/evansfrancis831

Instagram: https://www.instagram.com/evansfrancis831

Website: www.evansfrancis.org
www.evansfrancisbooks.com
www.christianappdevelopers.com

Email: contact@evansfrancis.org

CHAPTER ONE

CHOOSE YOUR GOD WISELY

For everyone who calls on the name of the Lord will be saved. (Romans 10:13)

Hello, sister! Greetings to you in the matchless name of our Lord and Saviour Jesus Christ! Let me remind you not to rush through this book but read it slowly. This will truly help you to always understand and retain the message in your heart.

My intention is not to get publicity but to convey the message God has entrusted me with. God has put a burden on me for the perishing souls of young sisters. My heart aches when I see them indulging in sinful acts. They get addicted to drugs, smoking, alcohol, illicit sex, and so on for fleeting pleasures. Instead of offering their lives as living sacrifices, they offer their time, body, and talents to the Devil.

One of the most painful and frustrating things for parents is watching their teens make bad choices and "throw it all away." Some of these choices include running with the wrong crowd, blowing off homework, dropping out of school, drinking, and doing drugs, and engaging in risky behaviour. However, if you follow the principles in this book, you will choose wisely and make your parents proud of you, my sister.

At first, many of the choices we make in life don't seem significant. But those choices set a series of events in motion that shape our lives and the lives of our children and grandchildren. The choices you make can lead to tragedy. Don't make them casually. Many girls' lives have been destroyed this way. For example, a girl decides to have a drink at a party. She lets down her guard, has no inhibitions, and ends up pregnant or with a venereal disease.

Since seemingly small decisions can have such a momentous impact, how can we protect ourselves from making the wrong choices? Lot's decision to move his herd to the fertile plain in the direction of Sodom (Genesis 13:5-18) teaches a crucial lesson about not judging things by appearances. Choose to follow the direction of the living God who causes your way to prosper.

When we read the book of Genesis, we see how sin entered the world. Adam and Eve disobeyed God and ate from the tree of the knowledge of good and evil, which God had forbidden them to eat from under the penalty of death (Genesis 2:17). Before eating the fruit from that tree, Adam was morally innocent. Nevertheless, when he partook, he became a sinner. As he sinned, he died spiritually, and the process of physical decay was set in motion

Adam was the first man on Earth. From Adam and Eve came all the families of the earth and every human being who has ever lived up to today. Since Adam became a sinner, every human being who descended from him became a sinner, except Jesus who was born without the seed of sin. Because of Adam's sin, death entered the human race too.

When Adam sinned, sin entered the world. Adam's sin brought death, so death spread to everyone, for everyone sinned. Yes, people sinned even before the law was given. But it was not counted as sin because there was not yet any law to break. Still, everyone died—from the time of Adam to the time of Moses—even those who did not disobey an explicit commandment of God, as Adam did. Now Adam is a symbol, a representation of Christ, who was yet to come. (Romans 5:12-14)

Since we are all born in sin, every human needs to be born again to be released from that nature of sin. To be born again is to know Jesus and make Him your Lord and Saviour.

As it is written in Romans 3:10: "No one is righteous—not even one." According to the above statement, no man seeks after God and no person does what is right. This means every man, woman, and child needs the righteousness of God, for without God's righteousness, no one can even enter God's presence. In simple words, every human needs to believe in Jesus Christ and be born again spiritually to be free from Adam's sin. We will remain spiritually dead until Jesus comes into our lives. Until that takes place, everyone is a sinner.

You might ask, what happens to those who believe in Jesus?

Abraham was saved because he believed in God. Noah and his family were saved because they believed in God. The thief on the cross was saved by asking the Lord to remember him when Jesus Christ returned to His kingdom—showing he believed that Jesus was the Promised One sent by God. All the apostles were saved because they believed Jesus was the Messiah (the Anointed One) sent by God. All in the book of Acts were saved by hearing and believing Jesus is the Christ (the Anointed One), the risen Saviour from God.

You know what, sister, I wasn't too close to God in my youth. But at the age of 20 when I believed in Jesus, I began to see a dramatic change in my life. I started to hate sin and began to live a life more pleasing to Christ. Once I made that decision, my life changed forever.

You may think you are the worst sinner on this earth. I used to think that too. My sins were that serious, and I felt I was of no use. However, the good news is no matter how great sinners we are, the blood of Jesus cleanses us of our sins forever. The next best thing is He forgets them perpetually, never to be remembered again (Hebrews 8:12).

Deciding to follow Jesus is the best thing you will ever do!

In the Bible, many had to decide whether to follow the Lord or not.

Adam and Eve decided to eat from the tree of the knowledge of good and evil.

Noah decided to believe it would rain and flood the earth; hence, he built the ark.

Abraham decided to leave his family and go to a land, which God would show him. Years later, he would offer his only son as a sacrifice to God.

Ruth decided to leave her family and friends and live with God's people.

Peter decided to deny Jesus, repent, and become a leader in the church as an apostle.

Judas decided to betray Jesus. He did not repent and ended up committing suicide.

Everyone has a choice: to follow and obey God or reject and disobey God.

What have you decided to follow, sister?

When you believe in Jesus, He enters your heart and transforms you into a totally new person. Even if you are addicted to drugs, alcohol, cigarettes, promiscuity, etc., you will be set free of all these addictions because Jesus died so you can live abundantly in Him.

Jesus has a plan and purpose for you according to Jeremiah 29:11:

For I know the plans I have for you,' says the Lord. 'They are plans for good and not for disaster, to give you a future and a hope.

Only through God's Word can you truly know and experience His plan for your life and His grace to live a new life.

Never think you are worthless. If you do, you will not be inspired to achieve anything. I know what it is like to feel that way, especially when I was weak in my studies. But it is written, God chooses the foolish to prove to the wise He is a living God.

The stone that the builders rejected has now become the cornerstone." This world might have rejected you, but God is enough to take you to new heights you may never have imagined. (Psalm 118:2)

Beloved, Jesus said in John 14:6, "I am the way, the truth and the life. No one comes to the Father except through Me" (NKJV). Jesus never said Mary and Me or Joseph and Me. It is only Jesus. He is the only way to heaven.

Beloved, you must receive Jesus Christ as your personal Lord and Saviour through faith:

God saved you by his grace when you believed. And you can't take credit for this; it is a gift from God. Salvation is not a reward for the good things we have done, so none of us can boast about it. (Ephesians 2:8-9)

When you receive Jesus Christ, you experience a new birth, the old [your name] is dead and the one who is alive is born again [your name].

There are four steps to becoming a born-again believer:

1. Repentance
2. Believing in Jesus
3. Baptism in water
4. Baptism of the Holy Spirit

Under the Old Testament order of law and sacrifices, whenever people confessed their sins, they offered sacrifices but then they often returned to their sins. However, in the New Testament, Jesus Christ became the ultimate sacrifice once and for all for our sins (Hebrews 10:1-18). Repentance is turning from sin and turning unto God. We must repent and believe in Jesus until our last breath. Why? Because we are all guilty in God's sight. Repentance comes before believing.

Repent ye and believe the gospel. (Mark 1:15, KJV)

We receive Jesus by personal invitation. If you would like to give your life to Jesus and allow Him to become the Lord of your life, say this prayer:

Dear Lord Jesus, come into my heart. Forgive me of my sins. Wash me; cleanse me and set me free. Jesus, thank You for dying for me. I believe You rose again from the dead and You are coming back for me. Fill me with the Holy Spirit. Give me a passion for the lost, a hunger for the things of God, and a holy boldness to preach the gospel of Christ. I am being saved. I am born again. I am forgiven and on my way to heaven because I have Jesus in my heart. Amen!

Amen! Amen!

Beloved, if you have said this prayer sincerely, from this time on, you have become the daughter of Jesus Christ. Your name is written in the book of life in heaven at this very moment. Note today's date because today, you have made the biggest decision of your life to live for Jesus. Congratulations! Welcome to the family of Christ!

CHAPTER TWO

Choose Your Friends Wisely

As iron sharpens iron, so a friend sharpens a friend. (Proverbs 27:17)

Everyone needs to stop and consider the importance of friends and the impact they have on one's life. God uses friendship as an instrument of sanctification. It is important that all Christians carefully choose their friends. In the past, I used to have trouble choosing friends. I'll tell you from my own experience, friends can either lift you up in life or pull you down.

There is an infinite number of reasons why we need friends. But here are just a few:

1. We need the love our friends have for us.
2. Life is more pleasant when we have those who care about us and our welfare.
3. We need to know there are those who love us no matter what. "A friend is always loyal, and a brother is born to help in time of need" (Proverbs 17:17).
4. Friends satisfy the need for someone to share our joys and happiness (Romans 12:15), the need for someone to

cheer us up in times of sadness (Proverbs 27:9), and the need to help us relax and escape the pressures of life.

The book of Proverbs is full of instructions concerning how we can do well and become successful, including how to choose our friends. Proverbs 13:20 instructs us to "Walk with the wise and become wise; associate with fools and get in trouble." Here we are warned that befriending foolish people is detrimental. It will bring harm to our lives. On the other hand, seeking wise friends who live right will bring many blessings.

Proverbs 1:10-16 gives a compelling warning against befriending those who engage in sinful lifestyles. The passage begins by saying, "My son, if sinners entice you, do not give in to them" (NIV). Solomon, the writer of those words, then describes the voice of these sinners. He says they will persuasively attempt to recruit you for a myriad of sinful or illicit acts, including bloodshed and theft (verses 11-14). In verse 15, he continues, "My son, do not go along with them, do not set foot on their paths; for their feet rush into sin, they are swift to shed blood."

Many times in the past, I allowed my friends to persuade me to go where I didn't want to and regretted it later. Be ready to say no to wrong. I know it is not easy to live differently from the crowd. Naturally, we want to be accepted and fit in. Today, what others say about you is considered more valuable than what God approves.

Dare to go against the grain of culture. Dare to walk the road less travelled. Dare to say, "No, I will not smoke, drink alcohol, smoke hookah or use drugs like others. I will not lose my virginity until I get married." I pray to God day and night to help me raise a generation like Daniel and his friends who had the boldness to say no.

The apostle Paul confirms the influence of bad friendships. He says, "Do not be deceived: 'Evil company corrupts good habits'" (1 Corinthians 15:33, NKJV).

This scripture and others indicate that to do well and be truly happy, we must follow the truth and obey God. Choose good, principled friends, and avoid negative, immoral people.

Friendship can have its negative aspects as well. So-called friends can lead us into sin. Friends can lead us astray regarding our faith. This is exactly what happened when Israel was led to worship false gods because of their surrounding neighbours. God had given them specific commands regarding idolatry in Deuteronomy 13:6-9:

Suppose someone secretly entices you—even your brother, your son or daughter, your beloved wife, or your closest friend—and says, 'Let us go worship other gods'—gods that neither you nor your ancestors have known. They might suggest that you worship the gods of peoples who live nearby or who come from the ends of the earth. But do not give in or listen. Have no pity, and do not spare or protect them. You must put them to death! Strike the first blow yourself, and then all the people must join in.

In the Old Testament, such acts of idolatry were punishable by death.

Beware! Our friends may not lead us astray, but they can provide false comfort and bad advice just as Job's friends did, making his suffering worse and displeasing the Lord.

When three of Job's friends heard of the tragedy he had suffered, they got together and travelled from their homes to comfort and console him. Their names were Eliphaz the Temanite, Bildad the Shuhite, and Zophar the Naamathite. When they saw Job from a distance, they scarcely recognized him. Wailing loudly, they tore their robes and threw dust into the air over their heads to show their grief. (Job 2:11-12)

Friends can also prove false, feigning affection for their own motives and deserting us when our friendships no longer benefit them.

It is not an enemy who taunts me - I could bear that. It is not my foes who so arrogantly insult me - I could have hidden from them. fellowship we once enjoyed as we walked together to the house of God. (Psalm 55:12-14)

Wealth makes many "friends"; poverty drives them all away. (Proverbs 19:40)

Many seek favors from a ruler; everyone is the friend of a person who gives gifts! The relatives of the poor despise them; how much more will their friends avoid them! Though the poor plead with them, their friends are gone. (Proverbs 6-7)

I have also seen many friendships broken through gossip (Proverbs 16:28) or grudges (Proverbs 17:9). In fact, I had a bad experience when one of my friends interfered in my life causing me to lose a beautiful God-given friendship. Always be careful that your friends are not any of the above, sister.

Note Jesus' example. Even with His disciples, He did not include everyone in His inner circle. This inner circle was made up of trusted friends, and He was careful about whom He included. He set a clear example for us to follow because He never allowed His destiny to be affected by His friends.

There is no escaping the truth of Proverbs 13:20: "Walk with the wise and become wise; associate with fools and get in trouble."

If you apply this principle and surround yourself with good, wise friends and associates throughout your life, you will reap limitless benefits in the form of success, happiness, and personal contributions to others. When I started to live my life like my husband, I felt closer to God, and I can feel God closer to me than ever before.

To surround yourself with positive people, consider implementing the following strategies:

1. Begin by replacing your negative or morally deficient friends with good ones. This might not be easy, but it is necessary to avoid being influenced by them to adopt non-Christian values.

1. Make a clean yet polite break from the negative group and then gradually make friends with people of high moral calibre and positive influence. These friends will elevate you to higher standards and help you reach your potential.

3. Beyond being blessed with positive friendships, resolve to be a positive friend yourself. Set a strong, godly example and be a light for others. In this way, you will also contribute to their lives and characters. Together, you will be able to fulfil the Great Commission given to us by Jesus Christ.

CHAPTER THREE

Choose Your Career Wisely

So, whether you eat or drink, or whatever you do, do it all for the glory of God. (1 Corinthians 10:31)

Decisions about our careers can sometimes be the hardest to make. For sure, it's very stressful, and on top of that, we never know if we are making the best decision for ourselves or not.

However, the Bible says successful people are those who serve God first, are of service to others, provide for family needs, and are at peace with themselves and the people around them. Regardless of the income, prestige, or security of a vocation, unless it truly merges with God's will, there will be unrest.

When you are choosing a career, your basic priority should be to glorify God alone. A job that requires making friends of a certain type might not be of God. Choose a career God has put on your heart, but above all, see that your conscience is clear. In other words, don't throw away your morals and values to advance your career or get a job.

God's will is for you to be holy, so stay away from all sexual sin. (1 Thessalonians 4:3)

When you choose your career, ask yourself one question: does this job fit into my overall strategy of building a Christ-like character? Your job should be one component of the strategy to grow more in personal holiness. Your career will define your destiny, so be very careful the choices you make, sister.

As God assures you in Psalm 32:8, He will guide you along the best pathway for your life. He will advise and watch over you. Always remember nothing is impossible with God. Learn to obey His voice. See to it your job helps you to grow in the Lord, rather than hinder your progress in recognizing the value of knowing Christ Jesus, your Lord. Always remember, a life not lived for God is not a life at all.

God paid a high price for you, so don't be enslaved by the things of the world (1 Corinthians 7:23). Do not choose a career that will make you a slave, so instead of God, you are obsessed with work. Work is important but not more important than God. Apply Ecclesiastes 9:10 to your life: "Whatever your hand finds to do, do it with your might" (NIV). Is this job worthy of your best effort?

After completing my education, I tried to get a job before I started my MBA. God categorically told me He was not sending me to study for the MBA like any normal person, but He was preparing me to be educated to be a helping hand in His kingdom. But I was not obedient to Him. I gave more heed to the voices of others. I took one job after another but never found the joy I used to have.

Later, when I submitted myself to God's hand, I could again experience His love, joy, and peace. Now, I can testify how wonderful it is to live for Christ. Looking back, instead of wasting my time, if I had been obedient to God from the start, I would have grown more in the Lord. I am sharing this because I don't want you to make the same mistake.

Follow God and don't try to please others.

Those lonely nights away from home were horrifying. Instead of God, I was engulfed in work, trying to be happy. Even though I knew God's will for me, I was not listening. Sister, if you know what God wants from you and ignore it, in simple words, you are going to make your life worse, just like Jonah.

The story of Jonah started out with disobedience. He didn't do what God wanted him to do and sailed away in a different direction. A storm came. The people on board threw Jonah into the sea to break the curse. A whale swallowed him. After some time, the whale vomited him out, and Jonah finally did what God wanted him to do.

Until we see God-sent storms as interventions and not punishments, we'll never get better; we'll only get bitter. Some difficult circumstances you're facing right now may well be God-sent storms of mercy intended to be His intervention in your life. The challenges we face may be calls to do something different, to do something better—to change direction.

Let your story be one of God's grace and deliverance, a story of acceptance on many levels. Let it be about accepting changes God guides you to undertake, no matter how challenging they may seem. Let it be about accepting God's grace as an individual and then not being hypocritical or hypercritical when others receive it.

When God asks you to do something, do it without question. Only then will you be able to see His hand working in your life, sister.

God has called you to a task just as He called Noah to build the ark. God called Moses and Aaron to their mission (Exodus 3:4, 28:1). He commissioned prophets such as Samuel, Jeremiah, Amos (1 Samuel 3:10; Jeremiah 1:4-5;

Amos 7:15) and others. He called Abram and Sarah to embark on a journey (which might be taken as a kind of workplace calling). He placed people in political leadership, including Joseph, Gideon, Saul, David, and David's descendants. God chose Bezalel and Oholiab as chief craftsmen for the tabernacle (Exodus 31:1-6). Jesus called the apostles and some other disciples (Mark 3:14-19). The Holy Spirit called Barnabas and Saul to be missionaries (Acts 13:2). All of them responded to the call. Will you?

Cease your anxious thoughts about your future and seize the opportunities God set for you. Ignore the temptation to make money your most important goal. Organise your life according to God's grace upon you as an individual and then commit yourself to your God-given calling and purpose in the field of work He assigns.

Making a career decision can be overwhelming without the Lord's guidance. It could be a part-time job or a full-time career—the most important first step must be prayer, seeking God. He may allow periods of unemployment in order to gather us closer to Him. Our responsibility lies in our willingness to trust in Him and diligently follow the paths He lays before us.

May God help you to choose the right career wisely. In Jesus' name!

CHAPTER FOUR

Choose Your Life-Partner Wisely

Society is buckling and crumbling under the weight of bad relationships. We've all heard the numbers and stories. The divorce rate is at 50 percent outside and inside of the church. Many boyfriend/girlfriend relationships end with each hating the other while carrying the baggage from the failed relationships into their future. So, choosing the right mate is crucial.

A marriage license is not a guarantee that the marriage will work any more than a driver's license assures you can drive cars. It merely gives you the legal right to try.

The righteous choose their friends carefully. (Proverbs 12:26a, NIV)

If you're expected to choose your friends carefully, you should be even more careful about who will be your life partner. Notice it is your choice. God doesn't do this for you. God wants you to make that decision. God leads us, guides us, and gives us timelines, but ultimately, we choose.

God doesn't tell you who to marry, but He does give you a description of the kind of person He desires you to wed. If you want God's blessings and protection on your marriage as well as success, listen to what He has to say about the kind of person you should marry.

Next to your decision to take Jesus Christ as your Saviour, the most important choice you will make is that of a life partner. Some people prefer not to marry. That is certainly acceptable, but most people choose to marry. Getting married is easy. But having a happy and successful marriage is another story. It is difficult. It is like working on a farm every day. One day is not enough.

Even though I got married recently, God has taught me simple but deep things about marriage, which I would like to share with you.

Biblical marriage is a lifetime commitment. It is a serious thing for a man and woman to solemnly vow before God, their families, and friends that they will love and cherish each other until death parts them. God takes all vows seriously.

When you make a vow to God, do not delay to fulfil it. He has no pleasure in fools; fulfil your vow. (Ecclesiastes 5:4)

God has no pleasure in those who make vows and break them. "I hate divorce" (Malachi 2:16).

Problems exist in any marriage. However, when both husband and wife know they are committed to each other for life, it is a big advantage. It provides a blanket of security and freedom in which they can work out their problems without the threat of divorce. In fact, the word "divorce" should never be used as a weapon in an argument.

What therefore God hath joined together, let not man put asunder. (Matthew 19:6, KJV)

Furthermore, it is never God's will for a Christian to marry a non-Christian; it's the same as being unequally yoked (2 Corinthians 6:14). Any Christian who deliberately disobeys the Lord's plain command and dates and marries a non-Christian can expect serious consequences. Having said that, it is not enough just to look for a Christian. You must look for someone who has truly committed his life to Jesus Christ, who has made Christ the centre of his life. Both husband and wife need to see the importance of giving Christ His rightful place in their lives and home.

Except the Lord build the house, they labour in vain that build it. (Psalm 127:1, KJV)

Again, I want to emphasise the fact that time is your best friend in determining if you are really meant for each other. Do not rush into marriage. According to statistics, the best time for men to marry is between the ages of 27 and 31; for women, the best age is around 25.

Take all the time you need to be sure you choose the right person but do not get engaged until you are prepared to marry in the near future. A long courtship and short engagement are better than the other way around. If you have to wait longer than a year to get married, then wait to become engaged.

I have known my husband for the last seven years. Yes, we have had our ups and downs, but one thing my husband always tells me is to live every day as our last. We are not guaranteed tomorrow; all we have is this day, and that is the principle I follow in my life. I choose to love my husband, take care of him, and stand with him as a strong pillar because that is what God has called me to be.

When a wife tries to become the leader in the household, that is where the problem starts. We both have roles to play. God designed us for different purposes. We don't have to do what God has designed men to do; we just need to fulfil our roles as wives. It's the simple things that make life.

My husband and I both have our grey areas, but nothing is hidden from each other. A great marriage is not when the "perfect couple" comes together. It is when an imperfect couple learns to enjoy their differences. The late Miles Munroe put it this way: "Marriage is two imperfect people committing themselves to a perfect institution, by making perfect vows from imperfect lips before a perfect God."— Myles Munroe, The Purpose and Power of Love & Marriage

A satisfying marriage with someone you love deeply is one of the richest gifts God can ever give you. If you think you have found your life partner, guard the sacredness of your relationship as you would guard a priceless treasure because that is exactly what it is.

Delight yourself also in the Lord, and He shall give you the desires of your heart. (Psalm 37:4, NKJV)

May God give you the wisdom and knowledge to choose your man wisely. In Jesus' name.

CHAPTER FIVE

INSPIRED MESSAGE

I hope this book has blessed you immensely. In this last chapter, I would like to share a small message from the Holy Spirit that inspired me. This is going to be small but powerful. If you obey all I advise, you will never regret your life, my sister.

My message is from the book of Ruth. So, after going through this chapter, read the book of Ruth. It will enable you to understand this message better.

Holding the family together when your world is falling apart is one of the greatest plans of God for you, sister. When we read Ruth 1:16-17, we can see how Ruth pledged her commitment to her mother-in-law without reservation. While verse 14 reveals her desire to care for Naomi, verses 16 and 17 reveal her decision. This passage is one of the most beautiful expressions of loyalty in literature. Its beauty and simplicity remind us of the characteristics of genuine commitment to a relationship.

It's the same type of commitment you need to show to God and the man you will marry. It is a costly commitment.

When Ruth was giving that commitment to Naomi, she was giving up her future. "Entreat me not to leave you." She pleaded with Naomi. She was willing to sacrifice her freedom for the responsibility of caring for Naomi. When Ruth's husband died, she was probably not more than 25 years old. For all she knew, she would never remarry or have children. But as a widow, she committed to caring for her ageing, widowed mother-in-law. This was a complete break with the past without any promises for the future. That is how you need to live your life for God.

When Ruth made that pledge to Naomi, she was giving up her own family. She said, "Wherever you go, I will go ... I will lodge. Your people shall be my people." She was leaving behind her mother, extended family, and friends. She was willing to sacrifice her national identity and homeland. She was leaving the land where she was born and raised, Moab, for a land with new and strange customs. Are you willing to sacrifice your family for the Lord? Which will you choose?

When Ruth was giving that commitment to Naomi, she was giving up her faith. She said, "Your God will be my God." She was willing to sacrifice her religious heritage and the worship of their idol, Chemosh, for the God served by Naomi. We would consider this her conversion. This was a costly decision. Are you willing to sacrifice your traditions for the Lord? Whom will you choose?

When Ruth was giving that commitment to Naomi, she did so for the long term. When you are giving your commitment to the Lord, it is forever until the end.

But the one who endures to the end will be saved. (Matthew 24:13)

Ruth's commitment to Naomi was sacred. She said, "May the LORD punish me severely, if I allow anything but death to separate us!" She didn't just make this vow to Naomi. She also made it to God. We still do this at weddings, so that we will remember God sanctions the home. By invoking the name of God, she made her pledge of commitment complete.

In short, she made a physical, emotional, and spiritual vow. There were no reservations.

Last but not least, Ruth proved her commitment:

When Naomi saw that Ruth was determined to go with her, she said nothing more, so the two of them continued on their journey. When they came to Bethlehem, the entire town was excited by their arrival. "Is it really Naomi?" the women asked. "Don't call me Naomi," she responded. "Instead, call me Mara, for the Almighty, has made life very bitter for me" (verse 21). "I went away full, but the LORD has brought me home empty. Why call me Naomi when the LORD has caused me to suffer and the Almighty has sent such tragedy upon me?" So Naomi returned from Moab, accompanied by her daughter-in-law Ruth, the young Moabite woman. They arrived in Bethlehem in late spring, at the beginning of the barley harvest. (Ruth 1:18-21)

Every year, thousands of couples pledge their love and devotion to each other, only to break their promises later. When you choose God, He will faithfully orchestrate His plan for your lives as He did for Ruth.

a. He moved at the right time

"They arrived in Bethlehem in late spring at the beginning of the barley harvest" (Ruth 1:22).

God's timing was impeccable. They, as widows, needed the springtime harvest (March-July) to sustain themselves for the rest of the year.

b. He moved in the right person

"Now there was a wealthy and influential man in Bethlehem named Boaz" (Ruth 2:1).

God intersected their lives with the one individual who could rescue them from their poverty. It was a godly relative named Boaz. We see God doing this throughout the Scriptures. It was no coincidence Philip met the Ethiopian in the desert. Likewise, the meeting between Ruth and Boaz was divinely appointed.

c. He moved in the right place

"And as it happened, she found herself working in a field that belonged to Boaz" (Ruth 2:3).

Someone wisely observed that nothing just happens with God. This, too, was more than a coincidence—it was providence. Do you remember the story of Jesus and the Samaritan woman at the well in John Chapter 4? Although the Jews typically avoided Samaritans, John 4:4 indicates that Jesus needed to go through Samaria. The story then pictures Jesus sitting at the well in Sychar as the woman approached and He was able to tell her about living water. This encounter changed her life and impacted the whole village.

d. He moved in the right way

"Then Boaz asked his foreman, who is that young woman over there?" (Ruth 2:5).

Widows were a common sight in the Jewish harvest fields. It was a provision of their culture to allow widows to pick up the fallen grain left behind by the harvester. But Ruth just happened to catch his eye. No doubt she was beautiful, but it is obvious from Chapter 2 that Boaz saw Ruth as someone special.

After reading the text, one cannot miss the invisible hand of God orchestrating this entire journey.

When Ruth chose God, God took care of the rest of her life. He brought the right person into her life.

- He was wealthy (Ruth 2:1).
- He was strong (Ruth 1:2).
- He was a considerate employer (Ruth 2:4).
- He was a virtuous man (Ruth 2:1).
- He was a man of faith (Ruth 2:4, 12).

While he was probably quite a few years older than Ruth, Boaz was Bethlehem's most eligible bachelor. So why had he not married? Nothing in the text indicates he was previously married. God was saving him for Ruth.

Do you remember the principle: "Your obedience to God's plan opens His provision for your life"? From the start of her life with God, Ruth demonstrated a consistent life of obedience. Disobedience would not have destroyed God's plan, but she would have missed God's best for her.

Notice the steps she took as God directed her.

- She believed in the Lord God (Ruth 1:16).
- She waited patiently (Ruth 1:22).
- She lived virtuously (Ruth 2:2).
- She was sensitive to God's leading (Ruth 2:3).

Whom will you choose sister, God or this world?

God is opening a path of great blessing for you. Receive it now. In Jesus' name!

www.ingramcontent.com/pod-product-compliance
Lightning Source LLC
Chambersburg PA
CBHW031650170726
47990CB00019B/3105